THE FOOL
IN
THE CORN

THE FOOL
IN
THE CORN

Tania Pryputniewicz

Saddle Road Press

The Fool in the Corn © 2022 Tania Pryputniewicz

All rights reserved. No part of this book may be reproduced or transmitted in any form or by any means without written permission of the author.

Saddle Road Press
Ithaca, New York
saddleroadpress.com

Cover art by Tania Pryputniewicz

Book design by Don Mitchell

ISBN 9781736525876

Library of Congress Control Number: 2022944023

Books by Tania Pryputniewicz
November Butterfly
Heart's Compass Tarot

Contents

Preface   9

I
Illinois: The Fool in the Corn

After the Overdose	17
Silhouette	18
The Ultimate Frontier	19
Kempton, Illinois: Tornado Watch	20
Chosen	21
Labor, Perkins' Farm	22
Firstborn	23
Lemurian Lovesong	24
Field Trip	25
County Fair	26
The Mothers of Stelle, Illinois	27
Harmless	28
Transgressions, or Bad Speller	29
Lemurian Nymphalidae, Square Dance Lessons	30
Normals	31
Recital: Canticle	32
Eva, Our Sitter	33
Cooking Class	34
Goat Milk Ice Cream	35
Swim Lessons	36
Bohemian Rhapsody	37
Blizzard	38
December at Mr. Gardner's Pond	39
The Fool in the Corn	40
Sea of Clouds	41
Lunar Maria, or Seas of the Moon	42

Fortune Cookie Proverb I 43
Frontier I 44
Couch Burning 45

II
California I: The Keeper of Keys

Catalyst, or Turning Eleven 49
Keeper of Keys: Schoolhouse Canyon, Russian River 50
Toad-face 51
Bus Stop, Hacienda Bridge 52
Free Box 53
Frontier II 54
Hades 55
My Geppetto 56
Moscow Road 57
Stepfather 58
Plainsong, After the Divorce 59
Fortune Cookie Proverb II: 60
The Page of Wands at the Wellness Fair, First Tarot Reading 61

III
Iowa: My Cocteau's Heart

Poetry Rules in the Heartland 65
Daughter of Egypt 67
Black's Gaslight Village 69
Vortex, or Fictional Daughter 70
Snowflake Bentley 71
Trading Readings, Or Toad Visits 73
Hall Mall, Iowa City 74
Rules for Consulting the Oracle 75
Batman 76
Graduation 77
Letter to the Queen of Swords 78

IV
California II: The Peacock in the Sparrow

When We Were Twelve 81
Morning Sickness 82

Bohemian Grove	83
Cookies, or the Three of Swords	84
The Marriage Counselor Channels King Solomon	85
Kolmer Gulch	86
Eclipse	87
Potato	88
Dropping in the Eight	89
Key	90
Opossum	91
Chocolate Rose	92
Daughter by Candlelight	93
Full Moon Ghazal	94
Spell	95
Chiron Return	96
Birthmark	97
Strength: Tarot's Arcanum VIII	99
The Daughters of Stelle	100
Fortnite Widow	101

V
California III: Berkeley Postcard

Berkeley Postcard	105
City of Metaphors: Six Months Later	106
Atrium	107
Chapel	108
Sanctuary	109
Sisters, or Waldo Pudding	110
Duck	111
Death Cocoon: Sister-in-law	112
Look, We Say, Look	113
Tarot Reading, Morning Before	114
Buddha Board	115
Visitors	116
Diana, Princess of the Amazons	117
Buddha Hindsight	118
Birthday	119
Eight of Swords	120
Closet	121

CLAREMONT CANYON HIKE	122
EMPEROR OF TRANSPORT	123
TWO GARDENS	124
THE KNIGHT OF SWORDS AND THE SIBLING TREE	125
TREE SYNCHRONICITY	126
NORWEGIAN AIR	127
MIRAGE	128
NOCTILUCA	129
LETTER TO THE EIGHT-YEAR-OLD LIVING IN THE CORN	130
GRATITUDES:	133
ENDNOTES	136
ACKNOWLEDGMENTS	139
ABOUT TANIA PRYPUTNIEWICZ	141

PREFACE

Out in the cornfields of Ford County, Illinois, where the redwing blackbirds sing, in the early 70s the city of Stelle – Latin for Star – bustled with construction along its newly formed streets and one cul-de-sac dubbed "the Crescent." Followers and their families came, drawn by a book, *The Ultimate Frontier*, by Richard Kieninger, telling how he came to be the Chosen and to lead the Chosen in an escape from imminent apocalyptic events. *The Ultimate Frontier* interweaves his universal history of spirituality with Kieninger's personal tale, including an initiatory experience in a cave. Whether Stelle in the 70s was a cult, a commune, or somewhere in between, the city attracted many earnest and loving families.

    Here, today, some fifty odd years later, I stand in my kitchen on a foggy Coronado morning, listening to my tea water roil and spit in the silver kettle, the clear lever at its base glowing blue, waiting for my youngest son to emerge in time to grab a bowl of oats and head out with his junior lifeguard fins. This life I've earned and shaped reopens with every page I risk writing. What were the Stelle years of my childhood for? What was my parent's marriage, if it ended in divorce?

    For years I accepted the Stelle experience as something that set my family apart. My parents chose to go to Stelle and took us with them. I didn't see it as my role to explain why we joined or why we left. As an adult, I understood my parents' desire to start over, following an accidental overdose my father suffered when he unwittingly drank an LSD-laced cup of punch at a Haight Ashbury party. And I understood their desire to raise children in a loving, intentional community. While I harbored reservations about men like Kieninger, who was expelled from the group for allegedly misusing his power with money and women followers, I didn't report much when asked about it. "We lived on a commune in Illinois. The world was supposed to end in cataclysms and there was talk of escape by rocket ship." The cataclysm part was true; I later realized the rocket ship was a myth passed between the children.

The children in the river town where we settled in California after leaving Stelle would respond "Cool," or "Weird," and then move on. Many of us lived in divorce-torn families that coped with alcohol or drug use, mental health challenges, and poverty. But even as my family merged with the "Normals" of the world, I took a particular way of seeing forward with me, a way I wasn't aware of for many years.

Stelle continued to thrive long after the leader was expelled. What follows houses my memory's re-imagining of my early years in Stelle's dream-field, leaving Stelle's dream-field, and sifting for the gifts that grew out of that brief but potent time in my life.

For my mother Mary, and my siblings, Peter and Rose Christine.

And for the children of intentional communities everywhere, especially the children of Stelle I grew up learning from, playing beside, and loving.

"For the Fool no difference exists between possibility and reality."

—*Seventy-Eight Degrees of Wisdom: A Book of Tarot*, by Rachel Pollack

I

ILLINOIS: THE FOOL IN THE CORN

AFTER THE OVERDOSE
[Utica, New York, 1972]

We keep our living room curtains drawn
until long after dusk. Father wakes to part them,

window's indigo glass rippling with night.
My brother and I stand beside him,

watching. Then our mother's footsteps
on the porch. In one hand a white bag

sags with donuts. Her sleeve is flecked
with fryer oil. Unbuttoning of coat, jangle

of keys in her fist, the kiss she gives us,
father last.

SILHOUETTE
[Stelle, Illinois, 1973]

Your father held you that January dawn,
knelt on the hospital lawn so you could hear the snow melt.

After the accidental overdose, he slept for a year —

leaving behind the apartment on Haight Ashbury,
its rooms painted black, balloons skirting the ceiling.

Silent his Beethoven on pink piano, silent his Peter, Paul,
and Mary on guitar, idle his hands whittling acorn kin
for us as we lay on our backs, lime paired elm tree seeds
falling into my hair.

Firstborn, passenger,

I inherit his love for the velvets of Cocteau, Bartok's
order of dissonance. My parents plan to start over
here on the commune, where the teacher

traces the shadow of my profile onto black paper,
cuts it from its page—as if taking a part of me—
tapes me and my brother at the end of the row

of side-facing faces of classmates we'll meet tomorrow.

Welcome to the fold,
the teacher says and turns out the lamp.

THE ULTIMATE FRONTIER

You were Pharaoh, King David, now our commune Leader,
trinity of selves in profile on the cover of the book

that drew my parents here. Though your title seems less a place,
more an unmapped psychological destination.

I dream my own potential past: Begin as Queen Nefertiti,
sidle back into my mother and arrive as me, waiting

in this Illinois room we drove through falling snow to reach,
where a little girl crawls barefoot under the oval table.

Above her on the glass, a purple math book. On its cover, a boy
framed by the porthole of a rocket headed for a city in the stars

I'll hear about in school, where we will eat sallow yellow wafers
for every chapter of subtraction, play chess, make paper airplanes.

You cross the room to greet us first – your Chosen Children –
passing harp, velvet curtains, daughter under table,

your wife in shiny pumps, every blonde hair swept off her neck
and cinched tight around a hidden comb,

neat lines of your suit, your hand coming down to grasp mine,
silver wake of your aftershave.

KEMPTON, ILLINOIS: TORNADO WATCH

Cellars fill with the fearful while I spin alone,
press my thighs into prickle of rope, ignore
the splinters of the plywood circle seat. June bugs thunk

out of the oak on their backs at my feet, their jointed
garnet legs rowing in symmetry. I've read the story:
Our Leader once met a stranger in a cave

who carved a design on his hip. How do you know
if you'll be chosen? Where your stranger will appear?

On Knox Street, beside the pink piano my father
rescued off a curb, his friends project home movies
onto a sheet in our living room

boat on lake,
boy on seat,
boy's thicket of arm hair,
ebullient maroon of mosquito's abdomen gorged with blood

while I sit on my mother's lap, snow-toes warm, ankles scuffed,
hours past bedtime. A gingerbread man cools on the stove,
an extra Red Hot – one of his buttons – stings my tongue
with its cinnamon glass.

Morning is a silver cone through which soybeans spiral,
ground into flour to float on the griddle. No maple syrup
can disguise the taste of field mold,

as here, none convince me off my father's swing,
his knot cinched fast beneath my seat.

CHOSEN

I believed you, Leader: The Elders chose you.
You in turn chose us. I bought Lemuria:
our collective past, filled in the rest.

Temples, cool basements, racks of honeycomb,
hearths wreathed in roses large as cabbages.

All the sentients, children too, cloaked in green silk,
like seedlings cohered around the axis of desire to reach the sun,

our sleeping pallets under starlight,
our trellises helixed with honeysuckle,

our coverlets soft as the ash-gold fur of the rabbits
chased by the mowers of the Normals
who tended the cornfields of Now,

past elms, damp dirt mounded between visible roots
upon which I stand, barefoot,

listening to the sons of the family from Switzerland
count down from ten
for the one last game of hide-and seek my mother allows,

the Northern Lights overhead
through which we'll surely pass on our way
to the city in the stars.

LABOR, PERKINS' FARM

Like a married couple or two husbands
my brother and I drive the dead tractors,
slicer-disks in rusty rows,
tires taller than our father or the farmer who owns it all—

our domain the open barn, dirt damp
with machine oil and the blood of headless chickens
scalded sterile and hung by bound feet.
My aunt rips quills off backs and wings, allows me a pluck;

the gizzard between my brother's lips
rasps and flutters with the force of his breath.
At moonrise, relatives disperse. As we range the dark lawn
voices rise inside the house –

Bedtime – my father hunts us in,
passing my mother in the kitchen.
The glance they share burns like a candle
melting its house to the ground.

FIRSTBORN

Coatless in the snow I hide behind the farmhouse. Whatever hunts my father
hunts my mother through him. I'm next.

Between empty cornfields and my body, on the only tree,
a snowy owl pivots her plush orb of head left,
quick right,

without altering her grip. I practice till the moon rises
and I no longer feel my feet.
Upstairs, my electric blanket crackles when I spin.

Brother in peripheral vision sparks too.
Under our beds, the dim twin dials blink orange.

I sweat in the wealth of heat,
dream of orphaned dwarves, underground suns,
black-eyed susans with their velvet centers brown,

petals wet. My father stands receiving,
his palms butterflied gold. What hunts us isn't him
but flows through him

as through the power lines overhead
on rows of parallel steel lattice towers
with outstretched limbs.

By morning I forget and the fear returns.
Oh Poppa, with your blue mantle of rage,
inherited, and no angel to carry it.

LEMURIAN LOVESONG

Through the tape-deck in my room
across the eons she sings: *War,*

plough, honey, and *bring him*
back home to me. Between bed

and ceiling, my body tight
as wrap-wire around steel,

one of six strings waiting
for the calloused hands

of the farmer's son to strum.
Outside, tall as rockets

the linked transformers
measure the acres like hours

until dawn along leylines
where the singer and her lover

once tended bees. Now we call it
Illinois, paint peeling on our cellar doors.

FIELD TRIP

    At the slaughterhouse,
    I believe the man in the blue smock,
    who promises to
    put the cow to sleep –

    mallet raised, cow's brown eye wet, nostrils flared,
    her outbreaths plumed like ours

    but what occurs
    is slam of mallet –
    buckle
    of forelegs, drop
    of hook from ceiling

    man's hands arc to winch
    the cow above us

    man's back blocks   [*cow split chin to gut*]   our view

    white blue   intestines   coil on the floor.

        When she wakes, let it be
        in unpeopled fields of green.

    One of my classmates raises his hand,
    "How many families will she feed?"

    I can write about it now,
    my daughter walking into my room
    to show me her bowl of seeds:

    Golden Acre, Giant Noble, Green Arrow
    and to ask, *would you mind if I plant some corn?*

COUNTY FAIR

Our Leader is, I begin to suspect, a man,
not a Messiah.

Holding my brother's hand in line,
I wonder if others see what I see.

Ticket bought, we mount the spoked wheel,
distracted by colored bulbs, mesh seat, chilled rims
of my ears
and the view
of the linear order of corn from the sky.

One more pass to touch the field
and up we go, a fraction closer to the stars
on our controlled and momentary arc of ascent.

By the time my body lets go
into the centrifugal force,
free of earth's gravity, we descend

past our mothers – lined up
as if for the Leader,
ready to hurtle sideways,

like Chagall's brides,
bouquets in hand, upturned faces rouged,
veils peeled and tucked behind their heads.

THE MOTHERS OF STELLE, ILLINOIS

Fireflies tip the kelp green grass as the beekeeper
threads the projector at sundown. Our mothers sit
in metal folding chairs, seat-weave's plastic white

frayed where fastened by rusted rivets. Hay
from the hayride in their hair, breaking
the dress code in their jeans, they clutch mugs

of spiked cider and ignore us. When Flash Gordon
soars across Judith's barn, every muscle visible
through his space smock—pretty as our Leader was –

they hoot and pull us on their laps. My sunburned
back stings against my mother's cotton blouse.
Her heart beats into my ribs under cover of darkness

as the fathers eat broken octagons of honeycomb
from lids of the film's silver canisters, propped
on the hay bales behind us. Flash in his one-man

rocket hurtles over the uncharted dunes of Mars
the patterns in the terrain strangely familiar,
our fathers watching our mothers watch him.

HARMLESS

That one forced kiss while she lay
anesthetized, awake, unable to speak.
He was one of many, she said.

That put him in context, ruthlessly.
How quickly she moved on to recall her ex
who *beat her within an inch of her life*.

She wore grey tights, a purple mini skirt
rimmed with a red stripe at the hem.
Their derision circled like a mobius

between them, their heads bent over
our kitchen table, knees touching,
hands clasped, my mother's unadorned

but for a wedding band, her friend's knuckles
topped with stones that looked like they hurt
to wear. She told of her car accident,

rhubarb red and green bruises, her left eye
puffed shut. *How dare he – Our Leader! –
kiss me when I couldn't move!*

        while I crushed Sanka grounds into the counter top.

TRANSGRESSIONS, OR BAD SPELLER

For arguing how to spell raccoon, we're sent to the Office.
I say two c's, he says one. My crime: not backing down,

his: spitting on my sandals and toes. *It's just as wrong,*
our teacher says, *to insist a fellow human being is wrong*

as it is to be *wrong.* But he *is* wrong: just last week
during Capture the Flag, he tackled me so hard

he bruised my kidneys, and now there's that bill to pay.
We sit in stalemate unable to apologize,

overlook the Crescent where the warty fairy slippers
of milkweed pods skim the sky.

He's an only child convinced he can always win.
I'm firstborn of three; he doesn't stand a chance.

Our war consumes us as the adults are now consumed,
weighing the character of our Leader in a trial.

Not over the plausibility of cataclysms we'll outwait
in starships, but over his advances to followers—

former wives in past lives, he explains.
Husbands in this life side with their wives.

And he's wrong about Doomsday, too:
sun rises, sun sets, and before bed, in my little blue book,

I track my good deeds +++

+ I told the bad speller I was sorry
+ I fed the outdoor cats
+I shared my Lite Brite with my sister

and the – –

– I hate the bad speller
– I re-bit the bite mark my sister left on my arm so I could show it to mom

careful to make sure the +++
outweigh the – –

LEMURIAN NYMPHALIDAE, SQUARE DANCE LESSONS

The Texan wife, our Heirloom butterfly,
curtsies to her man. Her petticoats prop her skirt

parallel to the ceiling, piñata lime,
her waist half the size of mine. Must we retreat

to the Valiant? I want to stay, watch her spin.
but down the steps to the parking lot we go.

On the radio: Henley's *Witchy Woman*.
I scan for her in the night sky, in the full moon,

the damp ditch air flanking the car, metered
by metronome of telephone poles   telephone poles....

Void of landmarks I count the road crossings
just in case

but my father knows the way –
almost home. In our Bermuda Triangle of corn,

a lone combine harvests harvested fields,
cablight lit like an angler fish

leading with his lure.
I stretch my hand out the window,

trawl the green night air,
convinced that the combine is driverless.

NORMALS

They were to be pitied – *unenlightened,
out of the know.* But I'd rather be them,

driving combines with colossal tires,
boots crimping the mud in miniature mimicry.

They fed their cows and tilled the land,
their wives made coffee and mincemeat pies.

Sons wasted neither milk nor hours
hunting for the Black Mentalists

we were told *required seven of their kind*
to align to destroy our planet. But fear not:

they could never agree on methods.
We had graver concerns, like stockpiling goods.

Forget the Mentalists! But how can I?
They're real as umbrellas to me: two feet tall;

when not lurking under our beds, they scuttle
through dusk's harvested fields to feed on stalks

of cane green bleached a mildewed gold
as they sift the rows for kernels of corn and teeth.

RECITAL: CANTICLE
—for Nancee

1.

She taught us first to look at her,
not mirror
nor door

where often stood her preverbal twins gripping the frame
and her husband with his grin,

as she in her Danskin and navy-blue tights spun across the floor,
auburn hip-length hair loosed of night's braids
rippling out towards him.

2.

There's a little rain coming through my window,
said the pig farmer to my father, averting his face.

Our beloved Nancee, freckles lining lips,
cued us to rise palm to palm

avoiding the eyes of fathers of friends
and men without children.

Afterwards, past fidgeting siblings and the velvet drapes
of the church auditorium,

a steady diagonal blizzard—the kind that stings the face
despite muffled burial inside a fake fur coat.

My ballet slippers slid across the parking lot,
rims of my feet scalded wet, haloed by red of taillights.

The country of snow bordering the windshield

re-portioned its fracture lines
all the drive home.

EVA, OUR SITTER

Eva unzips a pouch of tiny oval cases.
Every mirror doubles the glittering grids of color,

her curled palm warm and balanced against my cheek,
the doll-size brush tipped with azure,
her *wand of lunar snow*,
face inches from mine.

Look down, she says,
as she grips my chin with a smile,
one fingertip traversing my eyelid to blur the seamline
between two shades of shadow.

Look down, she repeats,
as if to say
forget the moments on the other side of this door

bordered by dress codes, formals,
field trip to a sewage treatment plant,
must-do homework on car-rides home.

She tilts my head, left, right,
then lets go to pick up her guitar, scent of cedar.

Her fingertips—still peacocked blue— hover
over the strings

sound hole's circle a portal
      through which both of us fly.

COOKING CLASS

Along her immaculate counter:
the silo of red-handled sifter, bright order
of silver spoons, lemon bales of butter

softening in late winter light. In cupboards
her husband the carpenter built,
bars of Baker's chocolate, dried figs,

quartered apricots and mason jars
of brined harvest. A good cook puts up her hair,
wears an apron, stores flour in her freezer

to keep boll weevils out, uses the shell
of her egg as a tool to separate yolk from white.
A good cook wears dresses, I learned

when I wore jeans one day and she sent me
home. She cited, over the phone
to my mother, the effect it might have

on her son, the kind of wife he might choose,
the man he'd become. My mother told her
I was not allowed to babysit for her again.

GOAT MILK ICE CREAM

When it is my turn to grip
the goat's warm and lumpy udders,
I pass, curl up on the braided
rag rug in the farmhouse cellar,

eye the garden on the shelves,
solar coins of carrots and
quartered spears of cucumbers
in forests of floating dill.

Judith – five boys, a baby
perpetually on her hip –
shows me where the pressure
cooker lid blew through the ceiling,

holds my hand so tight my mother
takes it back. *"Time to go home,"*
my palms red, sore from turning
the metal crank, throat numb.

I eat without shame each unfinished
portion the children leave on
the bench, undeterred by the musky
aftertaste and knobby head of

the giver of milk, her saturnine
green-gold eyes, her bleat insistent:
"Like me, Like me!"
Like Judith, on the front steps,

belled girl goat pacing her yard.

SWIM LESSONS

There's no ocean, lake or body of water
for miles in the corn but it's decided,
we should learn to swim. Mother yells, "Carpool,"

and into the Valiant we go, past borderless
clouds, pump-house red, juniper blue, berries
evergreen when halved by thumb. The changing

room chlorine stings; the lifeguard warns
he's seen lightning. We've wasted gas to get there.
We beg for hot chocolate and cinnamon rolls,

butter centers black with spice that burns
as it satisfies. Not today. We ride home
to the windshield wiper's glum refrain. Mother

shuts the door to her room, my brother and I
unable to keep quiet. Selfish. Hungry. Bored.
Through our half-open bedroom window,

a lightning bolt passes inches above our heads.
At midpoint spins a tendrilled orb lit from within.
I could reach up and touch it if only I would try.

BOHEMIAN RHAPSODY

Our parents left for the formal,
devilled eggs on a silver tray,
father minus beard,

our mother in white chiffon,
yolk yellow sleeves,
ringlets down her neck.

Must she go? Her perfume.
David's here – someone's son –
to babysit. A gust of winter air

over the row of empty boots.
A glimpse of stars, the prairie dark,
the obsidian bevel of the backdoor window

rinsed by headlights,
little brother bouncing on the couch,
their bedroom mine.

Radio on, standing on the bedspread,
slipping with that velvet singer into the mirror,
his blue bruised eyelids rimmed in glitter,

his maroon stenciled lips, his bare neck,
the epic grief, and the jury of the chorus:
the aching for the mother he betrayed

by killing another man. So many lives
before I chose this mother, this father,
the laws of separation set in motion,

five ironed blouses hanging in her closet,
her body dancing elsewhere without mine.

BLIZZARD

I want an indoor cat. The answer: No.
Two claim us anyway, one gray, one orange,
wreathing the side porch snow with their pawprints.

Seven days into the storm
snowmobiles cross our fields to rescue us.
Mom cries.

We travel in pairs; I hold the waist of a stranger,
someone Mom knows from the restaurant
where Dad agreed she could waitress on weekends.

Blankets, hot soup, cereal between meals,
the alien thrash of a television set,
the gunshots of Westerns, the smell of coffee,

women's voices in the kitchen. Mom smiling.
I don't know what to say when addressed,
my shyness a cylinder that recedes when I'm alone.

Startled awake, as if still in my farmhouse bed,
I fear for the cats. We return; search the farm
to cornfield's edge.

Two days pass before they emerge
through a curtain of falling maggots
when we lift the trash trunk's lid –

survived, Dad says,
by eating down garbage, closing themselves in.

DECEMBER AT MR. GARDNER'S POND

Winter pharaoh reigns; prairie wide his sphinx,
geode blue the miles of snow by moonlight.
His Egypt is my heart. In it first lived

my brother who followed me into the grove
where Norwegian Pines swirled in pairs, violet
trunks beneath our palms. Knee to knee we hid

under the lowest bough's centrifugal hem,
our breath plumes joined until our parents passed.
Furred bulrushes marked the border of the pond,

adrenaline's plural darts, obsidian as the tailed
pollywogs that fled our shadows by summer,
and lovers years later I'd grieve leaving.

THE FOOL IN THE CORN

    I woke on your birthday
            in the empty farmhouse
        forcing last year's kernels from their bed of cob –
              some indigo, some maroon –
        each hull white as sunlight in the barn

    scissor's silver loop cold against my thumb
            like windows crossed with furred stars of frost
        in bleating ranks advancing like the beating
            of owl's wings beneath the rafters
        and over the lawn – soft, imprecise

    unlike the decisive shear through the cloth on my lap
            or the fantasy of Pharaoh's daughter
        and a portal to the Nile behind the rusting combine,
              its corrugated hanging door streaked
        with the dank orange of duck eggs

    our mother shamed you for throwing last spring – *Destroying* –
            she shook you – *don't you see?* – *the circle of life*
        she needed you to respect, just as I need you
              to wake to a gift in our house of winter cupboards
            where mice litter the shelves with droppings like black rice.

    I listen like Joseph to my dreams, wonder which one
            will change our fate. Until then, little brother,
        I've sewn our fortune – a cupful of corn –
              into three hand-size pillows
        you can throw and retrieve.

SEA OF CLOUDS

    From here on Earth, Moon's half-dome floats to the left.
        My shoulder touches my brother's
        as we lie on the farmhouse lawn, disappearing clouds:
Choose yours. Close your eyes.

    Focus: fringe of shifting edges and pale sky sparking white.
        Then the gapped black of trying too hard,
        as when guessing the color you send me:
Butter, I say – not *yellow*, but close enough.

    Just as it matters more – this hour with you, little brother,
        than how our skills might later be employed.
        Time enough to wonder in another season,
after the auroras descend in winter

finding us here again on our backs,
        pressing tandem angels into snow
        with just enough wing-strokes to leave an impression
floating above the dead lawn.

LUNAR MARIA, OR SEAS OF THE MOON

The cataclysms never came. Our Leader voted out,
separated from his wife. The new man: wise, kind, good
from his freckled toes to the roots of his sandy hair.

On a sleepover with his daughter, I hid her gerbil
in the silverware. When I separated the tail
from the rump with the sliding drawer's accidental slam,

the mother cleaned the trails of turds and drops of blood
off the spoons and butter knives without reproach.
I read the *Diary of Anne Frank*, wondered

what part of history would repeat – who would want us?
Where would we go? Wondered how you befriend
the Normals we would leave behind – when they lived

everywhere, in town after town—from the Crescent
to New York to the right, California to the left.
Wondered why are the moon's asteroid craters

called seas. You can visit anywhere in a dream,
even these waterless seas – the poetry of names
doubling the distance between here and reality:

Sea of Nectar, Sea of Clouds, Sea of Serenity,
Sea of Crises, Sea of Tranquility. Lunar soil powdering
my feet, our empty kitchen cupboards back on Earth.

FORTUNE COOKIE PROVERB I

Not every closed eye is sleeping...
just ask the glassblower
living above her kiln

to better hear the pace of its flame,
ever ready to feed the fire
or damp it down.

I yearn to stay in her windy, salty city
but my father and the piano shop owner
decide there's no work

so back to the commune we go.
I too listen in my sleep—
not for fire but for the sound of shifting

continents. In the velvet gap
before dream, our journey repeats:
the artist's hands, the blowpipe spinning,

tipped with molten glass,
the vase she forms, brined
with her trapped breath.

FRONTIER I

On the commune we all sought it:
the something more. The painter
didn't find it and left.

Before that,
he sketched my father's face.
The likeness, framed and hung,

amplified Dad's omniscience,
iris of eye watching mine –
fine graphite strokes

like sunrays
forming orb around the pupil
made of absence – white of paper

– a restlessness with the present,
us and our mother in it.

I read late, convinced I might learn
to vault away
into other incarnations –

like Oversoul Seven –
if only I could find the door.

COUCH BURNING

Behind the farmhouse it awaits its death,
cushions stacked over kindling, a red can
of gasoline, and two wives who haven't left

the commune yet, come to say goodbye,
with casseroles, Corning Ware, rimmed
in cornflowers mazed by rootlets of baked oil.

I love its coarse maroon velvet prickling
my palm, the bald canvas paths my fingers trace:
leaves to stems to massive leaves again,

hours reading the Le Guin book my parents
argued about behind closed door, then
to my face, then gave in, in which

the *he* becomes a *she* in certain seasons
to lie with a lover. Something warm to cling to,
night after night, soothed by their foreign worlds

while this one breaks. In the morning, fabric singed
from frame, coiled black springs welded fast
in a row like sisters, ribs exposed, circle over the coals.

II

CALIFORNIA I: THE KEEPER OF KEYS

CATALYST, OR TURNING ELEVEN
[California, 1978]

The cats are left behind. The bribe: *the mountains,
redwoods, and sea will awe you.* Unspoken:

this move will save the marriage. A maroon
57 Chevy, three children in the wooden camper

my father built, the Illinois farmhouse empty,
tablecloths left tumbling in the dryer.

A month's drive to California, tracking inflections
with the acuity of the eldest.

Beside the grey of San Francisco's sea,
our dented hubcaps spiral into sand.

Fishermen lean in pairs against the stone wall
and watch my father dig us out.

She says they lost sight of a common goal.
He says he wasn't sure, deep down, he loved her.

KEEPER OF KEYS: SCHOOLHOUSE CANYON, RUSSIAN RIVER

On the third day of rain we wake to wet feet in the loft,
our wooden camper parting at the seams. Its pine siding
is varnished blonde, maroon letters stenciled in an arc:

The Piano Doctor. In a blue flannel nightgown
I run through eucalyptus to the campground bathroom,
mosquito hawks circling the lime fluorescent lights

where I brush my teeth with strangers. My father
has a piano to tune; on the way, I tell him my dream:
a narrow hallway of locked drawers, a keeper

with a ring of keys she hands me to open at will
the life after life I'd lived. "Did you hear?"
my father says to my mother, "We dreamed

the same dream!" My mother gazes out the window
at the rows of children under umbrellas, all
the other mothers in spy coats white, green, pink,

pristine as Holland tulips. When the bus arrives,
I want to stay with him, go with him to listen
for the familiar incessant gong of repeated tones,

each string tuned to the one behind. The dream
of the key keeper with her illusion of choice
remains close, until I step out of the truck

and run in yesterday's wet clothes to chorus practice
where I stand on the bleachers behind the sopranos,
their hair perfumed, their socks lace-trimmed.

TOAD-FACE

That's what the father called his five-year-old son
at the campground. The boy repeated it back.

My brother, sister and I — my parents too —
snickered. Just poison oak and a few redwood

seedlings between our sites. We searched
for kindling. Dusk darkened and so did

the tone of voice, the o in *Toad* exaggerated,
the c in *Face*. The mother joined in.

But we were none to judge, three weeks in,
posing as campers, waiting for my father's

piano shop check from Illinois. Soon the owners
would park us on the back road for free, loan

my mother twenty dollars for bread. But tonight
we emptied our canned stew into our tin cups,

grateful to be us, tried not to stare at the child
clutching his stuffed snake. His father's face

morphed in the firelight, green shadows
overtaking his throat, tongue spiraling out

to snap at a marshmallow blackening
on the end of a stick.

BUS STOP, HACIENDA BRIDGE

In line in the rain behind me, the football jock
Turnbull asks what I'll be for Halloween.

I say, *A fairy*, a-shiver with visions of russets
and wands. When he says, *Perfect!*

You are such a fairy! I'm elated that someone
so popular sees past my peeling tennis shoes

and the red skirt I wear all month in the campground.
Later I realize he meant it differently – that here,

men in four-wheel drives, baseball bats hidden
under seats, hunt lovers – other men – for sport.

I wonder who else is hunt-worthy and why.
I miss dance class, the feel of new recital tights

Capezio pink, the white kidney bean cardboard
soles of ballet shoes, the simple cotton cord

curling tight to pucker their leather shut,
the thin elastic band snug over the top of my foot,

the sound of padded feet moving over the floor
as we warmed up without music, without wings.

FREE BOX

I wait until she leaves the laundromat –
the pretty girl with long blonde hair

I've seen in the hallway at school.
The skirt is beige with pockets, gathered

at the waist, ankle-length, and has a peach
silk lining. The invisible zipper still works.

I turn it for stains – none – roll it
into a ball and tuck it at the bottom

of my pillowcase while my mother
talks to a lady about what it's like

living with us kids in the truck.
I take care not to wear the skirt at school;

on weekends I scan the store aisles first.
When we left the commune, no one said,

"This is true," and "This is not." No one said,
"This is yours," and "This is not."

Somewhere between "imminent cataclysms"
and "neither the gentle Lemurians

nor the brilliant Atlanteans made it"
I must find my way. A free skirt is a start.

Beneath its simple tan cotton outer layer,
silk fit for a queen of Egypt sheathes my thighs.

FRONTIER II

The painter and his family visit. My mother
offers to sit for him; a canvas we can't afford.

By now both of my parents have had affairs.
The woman's palm supports her chin;

vines in the pattern of the chair trail out
of the fabric's border to form a trellis in the sky.

By now I know that it's a lie: you live
one incarnation at a time. An older boy

starts a rumor at school: we kissed, he says,
under the pink canopy of my princess set —

gold and white vanity and mirror, the gift
of a girl up the street. I don't ask

to be chosen nor do I stop him. I will the wall
to answer, implore: *show me Oversoul Seven's door.*

HADES

We were all Eurydices back then,
and in love with one another's brothers.

Before boys, the plastic Palomino
on windowsill, seamline sharp
down gut, sentry of the dewy
indigo panes, curtains parted.

Before horses, Paint By Number
with contour map of blue ovals,
linked plastic pots propped open
like the keys on a sax.

Before art, the goldfish gorging itself
on pastel flakes we pinched over
the rim until his mouth ceased
trailing beads of air.

Before mistakes, falling asleep
to father's piano, unaware
we'd have to play all the parts:
boy, girl, even lover's harp –

cold as the metal gate
on the horse ranch, headlights
of my brother's truck, my girlfriend
choosing him, her hands

in her back pockets as I walk
the gravel lane to the main road alone,
the sound of ocean to the left, stable
half-doors closed, all the horses in.

MY GEPPETTO

My father's stain-striated thumbs bleed maroon,
scalded by stripper from refinishing antiques.
He tunes a piano a day by ear.

He lifts the action out of a Steinway,
black apron with a stitched golden harp on the pocket,
row of nested two-tan hammer paddles

mute as spindled uteri waiting for hips in a marionette
factory. At the monastery, Brother Felix ambles
towards Compline with his guitar as the monks

in oat white robes line up along the nave,
baritone voices mingling around the note he plucks
for them to find before they begin to sing.

What question can I ask that is worthy of my father's time?
What answer accept?
Busy as he is with the spine of sound, hours of practice

between us, from Bartok to the Escher-like precision
of Bach's Preludes and Fugues. He rummages drawers
in search of the perfect collar of felt.

Why did you fall out of love with my mother?

MOSCOW ROAD

We're white as the seats in the Camaro speeding down
the wrong side of the road. It's the year of the divorce,
the new man's house – his rules, his chair, his cuts of meat

bleeding into butcher paper. My brother fries up liver
in defiance, blends protein drinks with ground bull balls,
works out at the gym, disappears after he is caught

with his girlfriend in our mother's new waterbed. I fought
for this ride, brought the city boys to the door so my mother
could ask their names and shake their hands. Maybe she read

it would make them behave, in one of the books she kept
in the bathroom, *Cinderella Complex, My Mother My Self.*
I read them too, Erica Jong's "zipless fuck" contextless

before sex. My best friend in the front seat wears no seatbelt.
The boy I have a crush on is next to me in the back, cologne
and gold cross on a chain I confuse with a holy heart.

Heart on the radio belting *Barracuda*. The boys pour us vodka.
The amber spokes of redwood trunks and green leaves pass
in one continuous blur punctured with white lights of trucks.

I pray to the Angel of Death: *Let me walk from this car,
take me back to my father's house*; on his shelf, *Life after Life,*
its Jackson Pollack cover a haloed orb like a cell dividing.

STEPFATHER

She divorces you after our father, expects us
to divorce you too. But we can't, my sister and I,

our drawers full of you, a dozen or more
of your worn cotton T-shirts, burgundy and blue,

snuck one by one from your dresser
mornings you worked construction,

stepping over last night's oil-stiff jeans
and tar-stained boots, pennies and dimes

spilled round the base of your five-gallon coin jar,
your new Louis L'Amour on the nightstand

beside your glass with its half inch of melted ice
and Jack Daniels, refrigerator stocked with meat

wicking into its butcher paper sheathes.
So different from our father, under whose roof—

when tunings ebbed – we lived on puns
and hand-harvested puffball mushrooms

folded into omelets, Bela Bartok, the free gold
of the Aurora Borealis. On my father's workbench,

the promise of rent money: fairy red strips
of felt woven over and under silver strings,

hammers tight and even. You kept us in tennis shoes.
Our father stood in your doorway – our doorway now –

thanking you. You always rose,
shook his hand, and thanked him for the gift of us.

PLAINSONG, AFTER THE DIVORCE

Defunct in my father's house, four amber columns
of water rise from the floor to the ceiling to gather
sunlight though they fail to heat our rooms.

He pays for piano lessons, listens in. I begin
with *Canticle*, thinking *heart of the flower*,
learn it means song, hymn, prayer. Pray

help me remember the order of notes. U's of vines
vein the basement wall, root runners thin
as the aqueous trills of unseen sparrows.

The fan's mahogany blades serrate cobwebs.
By night, moonlight – diffuse, backlit with a blue
I crave – crosses the sill without the moon.

I can't stop wanting you to pull me starward,
all cells singing until the body's grief disintegrates.
In my future, on a shelf, the Tarot waits,

twenty two soul cards, beginning with zero,
the Fool, who does not know what questions lie
in her satchel, nor their answers that can only be lived.

In my future, I'll enter the deck alone, trust
the voice – familiar, quiet – and hear
with peripheral ear the canticle of the heart.

FORTUNE COOKIE PROVERB II:
[Psychology 101, UC Davis, California]

To hypnotize the willing, the TA pays
ten dollars a session. I pedal a stationary
bicycle in a lampless broom closet

as he counts backwards from ten.
I do not experience any shift
in consciousness, Tart's *Altered States*

on our syllabus, nor do I find the shepherd
of this incarnation, not even Oversoul Seven,
just a memory of another blizzard

approaching the farmhouse, my brother
separating cerulean marbles from clear
for one more game of three dimensional

tic tac toe in three planes of glass, moored
by narrow silver columns
to form a see-through house without walls.

Land, says my fortune cookie,
is always on the mind of a flying bird.

THE PAGE OF WANDS AT THE WELLNESS FAIR, FIRST TAROT READING
[UC Davis, California]

Under fluorescent glare,
between the blender display and the seed catalogues,
    a woman shuffles
        a deck of cards.

My friends pass her, but I stop, pay,
sit on the cold metal folding chair.
    Each card-back
        bears the same pattern:

blue mountaintops
tree tips
    drowned steeples,
        scales of a leviathan fish –

a Pied Piper's hidden door.
This is you, she says, after laying out the deck,
    face up –
        our Querent of Now –

and it begins:
the descent into the Page of Wands
    and her land
        which I can occupy at will:

snug hat, scarf at neck, vest threaded shut with a leather cord,
cattails behind left shoulder,
    a blossoming walking staff
        inscribed with rowan berries.

You must bring back, without apology, all that you dare.

III
IOWA: MY COCTEAU'S HEART

POETRY RULES IN THE HEARTLAND
[Iowa City, Iowa, 1992-1994]

I.

The land – the corn itself – triggers
the panic attack. Miles of dank green leaves
cup stems in field after field around
the classroom.

Fourteen years since the commune
and I've survived, earned
this spot in seminar. The others introduce
themselves, mention the right poets.

I list a book on the afterlife
and Dion Fortun's *Mystical Quabalah*.
During critique it is established
that past lives don't grant you permission

to speak with authority
from that life's point in history;
that if your father tunes pianos, it's best to use
metaphors of the tuning fork.

*Where else if not in poetry might past lives
find witness*, I wonder –
but listen, outlier in a new field
of corn. At night I dream

with the velocity of a shaman's apprentice,
only there's no shaman I trust
nor do I wish to be anyone's prophet
but my own.

II.

I meet Jane the Visiting Poet on the street
while the dusk rain fastens gingko fans
and a sparrow to the sidewalk at our feet.

We agree I'll take in the bird. In my basement flat,
a coiled bent metal arm holds up the hot
second sun of my writing lamp. Sparrow

rights herself, tiny stars of feet against my palm,
brief heft of her body taking to the sky
at the stair top like Jane reciting from *August Zero*

by heart at the faculty reading, pacing the rim
of the stage curating an adrenaline
vacillating between fear she'd forget a stanza

and fear she'd fall into our laps. Later,
as my thesis advisor, she'll remind me,
"You chose to be an artist so you could be free."

DAUGHTER OF EGYPT

I.

Unclaimed in a rented farmhouse
without insulation, my brother and I made
paper tickets for a circus we peopled

ourselves, doubling as trick and crowd.
Above us, the limitless auroras
and winter's perpetual violet dusk,

a threshold I trespassed at will to reach
any other time but the present. Egypt was
our heritage: I still believed the Leader.

When a hawk dropped a rabbit on the eaves,
I learned that what you hunt should weigh
no more than what you can carry.

When half the group left with the wife,
I pitied the Leader. In class we made
dioramas of the Nile, painted boys

in kimonos. As I spun for my mother,
pins in the seams of my red
velvet dress beaded my sides with blood.

II.

In graduate school the poet challenged
my love for the ethers, the invisibles,
by following me twice.

Once into a dream,
where she laid a red cape down
over a stone wall
so I could cross into the woods.
And once by day,
where she advised me,

Put the sun back in the sky of your now,
allow the rays of its light
to fall onto the world before you —
the trees, the grass, the faces
of the ones you love —

before you track the shadows
cast by a source of light
in a world you cannot name —

a world like the one I had yet to leave,
where the lids of indigo sarcophagi
glinted with the honey of desert bees
and gold of lions.

She was right: the only world
is the world we share — forgiven, all:
Leader, father, poet.

BLACK'S GASLIGHT VILLAGE

lies on a psychic faultline, inducing bouts
of lucid dream. Iowa's night rain thrusts
onion grass level with my basement screen

in triplet sheathes. My carousel of selves
spins: merfolk to salamander to androgyne
shaman. Last night I fell, a 13th century child

trapped beneath rubble of a church. On waking,
I climb down the loft's ladder, but am pinned
by caring for others' grievances.

At first, I don't believe my therapist
when she says I can control my dreams,
or stop hemorrhaging time to others in need.

On my altar I rest the Two of Disks: Cobra
curled in a figure eight, pale green skin gemmed
with pastel diamonds. Crowned king of himself,

he bites own tail as if to curb forward motion –
as I do – to revisit the past. Within hours my cat
drops a snake on the snake on the card. I clean away

the blood, bury the snake, try to decide which metaphors
belong to dream and which I seek…and which,
if I'm not careful, my little listener will bring to my feet.

VORTEX, OR FICTIONAL DAUGHTER

The break in serial lovers occurs after months
of ignoring the therapist and her literature,
of part-time work at The Vortex Crystal and Gem:

floor sales, mailing list updates, helping the book buyer
select merchandise. Such spiritual playgrounds
attract as many confused souls as the commune.

I'm at ease amid amber necklaces, boulder-sized
Buddhas, their rosewood auras oiled and burnished
by hand. Silver dolphin gyroscopes spin beside rows

of books by Walk-ins, Bone-Knitters, Pyramid Sitters,
Aura Readers and Angel Healers whose talks we attend
at a discount. I love best the last two hours, customers

banished, the vacuum's gritty snuffle of miniscule gem
flecks under the mineral display beside the greeting cards.
Our handsome employer – default Father – trusts us to it.

His wife – Mother – owns the adjoining restaurant,
The Kitchen, where I, fictional daughter,
take my paycheck or Tarot cards to read

in exchange for Pasta Primavera. Mother grants me
a booth for clients. They bring their cold hands,
their childhoods, a ferocity of longing I ply

armed with my heart, my voice,
my deck of brightly painted cards.

SNOWFLAKE BENTLEY
—*for Wilson A. Bentley, 1865-1931*

He waited hours
in the open barn
for the optimal chill, angle of light,

rate of snowfall needed
to intercept
each single snowflake
on a pitchfork's tine

in time to transfer from tip
to swath of velvet.
Then the rush
to photograph, camera rigged
to his microscope:

pages of rows of white
micrographs
on a black backdrop
he called miracles
of beauty, ice flowers.

Two weeks after
Snow Crystals was published,
walking in a blizzard,
Bentley caught pneumonia
and died.

He was the first
to guess no two snowflakes
were the same.

Keith Jarrett,
during his Köln concert,
on the battered rehearsal piano
he was forced to play,

returns to the same
note over and over –

yet no two sounds alike —
subtlety of wrist, rhythmic knock
of sustain pedal —

And unbidden, intermittent —
the passion of his vocalizations
indelible.

TRADING READINGS, OR TOAD VISITS

When the book buyer gifts me a sample deck
I shuffle through: *Lion, Bear, Snake* –
face-up before turning it over to choose my Totem –
Oh, Dove, Fox – anything but Toad, please!

For he's mud-moss green with a dull oblong
garnet over his third eye.

Too proud to return him to the deck, I work
to connect with my Inner Toad, signifier
of "Eternal Beauty," "Hidden Wealth,"
"Sensitivity to Poison," like "toxins found
in underground streams."

Several towns away, where I read Tarot cards
on weekends, the Palm Reader suggests a trade:
I'll read for her daughter, she'll read my palm after.
Her daughter confides, cries,
and the Palm Reader lingers in the hall,
pacing, as if I've overstepped.

She grips my palm with cold hands,
lacquered nails, says my future husband –
when I finally find one –
will certainly not always be faithful.

We are professionals; I hate to cry but do,
hives breaking out along my neck.

I drive home at dusk under a thunderstorm's
dark blue. The rain evicts miniscule hoppers
that clot the two-lane road. I ferry dozens across.

Their tiny haunches spring relentlessly –
jut and thrust of each determined chin
from my palm to my arched fingers
and back – until I free them
into the rising waters of the ditch.

HALL MALL, IOWA CITY

The White Brotherhood is the topic of a talk
you, Leader, will give in Chicago, says the ad
in a donated zine my friends and I priced at a dollar

at The Secret Goldfish where we sell used art.
We take turns running the shop, listen
to the silversmith across the hall fit his customers

for rings. The store to the left is lined with buck
knives and blacklight posters. So I didn't, then,
invent you, or my family's years on the commune.

Did you tell the story of the cave, the carving
on your hip, how the Brothers chose you to lead?
That day I scoffed, kept the zine to show

my girlfriend. Now I too omen hunt, though
I don't call it religion, nor build airships
to wait out cataclysms, nor kiss the wives

of my querents. I am likely older now
than you were then. I feel it too – the sweet
periphery, adrenal surge of possibility,

as when a Tarot card "talks" and an unexpected
answer voices itself in response to a hidden
question, a doubling of time and space,

as when sunlight rims my young son's hat,
frail haloes of pale Forget-Me-Nots across
his bare shoulders in Milky Way—wide swaths

arcing through the green ditches beneath
the redwoods. I am just a woman walking home
with vegetables to cut on my cutting board.

RULES FOR CONSULTING THE ORACLE

When gamblers ask which horse to back,
or jilted lovers expect us to eavesdrop

on their exes in the astral, it's wrong –
a string plucked darkly on the dark harp

housed in the human heart. It hurts to turn away
shy boys in love with girls long lost or never

approached, but I can't in good conscience
accept more dollars to deliver the same message

in slight variations of the cards.
I wrap my Tarot decks in silk, hide them

under my bed, hold fast to my mentor's rules:
Never attempt to discern the state of a third party

without their permission, nor consult the oracle
for gamble or profit. Should you discover

you are the hunted – as is prone to occur
in games of projection – remember the game

is yours to end, players yours to escort to the door.
A fourth visits in dream, all gesture:

a leviathan indigo mare with a red mane,
orb of her obsidian eye reflecting mine.

BATMAN

Walking home after the movie, I enter the set
of the rain-wet street, orphaned, fall

into the cave to the uprush of displaced wings.
Except I'm the girl, object of desire, not

the boy with a secret identity who can avenge
the past. I've stood in crowds of familiars

and crowds of strangers, echolocation
disabled. This time the old easy divisions

fail. It's possible I'm the one living
in the cave, alive and alone, kin hidden

but present, wings mine. And safe inside
a flat on Morningside Drive, guitar on my knees,

I'll sing to the silver tabby sitting at my feet.
He'll listen, hunt while I sleep, deliver

to my pillow: a furred, slender, dusty
black mound still warm, with curved slips

of ears lined with amber tufts, tiny elbows
ensconced in wings I'll unfold. My body

this fragile, uncloaked, this arrested – sure
I could soar if returned to the hour before.

GRADUATION
[1994]

Bless the Iowa River, accepting without complaint
the watermelon, strawberries, half gallon of honey,
the cantaloupe halves listing seeds.

Bless the bridge swallows arcing without colliding
through pillars every dusk. Bless the snow days
throughout the long winter afterwards,

substitute teaching, the counties phoning in
on the radio by district: Mid-Prairie, Mount Vernon,
West Liberty, West Branch. Bless the secondhand

armchair, worn lion-gold velveteen, a book
off the bargain table from Prairie Lights. Bless
the charts of the Famous you're handed without names

when you walk in the door. Bless the shock
of recognition, Plutonian clarity, Marilyn Monroe's
planets, the familiar in a new landscape,

as when, as a Midwest Bride floating in Fiji
above divers for the first time, silver coins
of escaped air mingled with your hair

like the currency of corn filling silos.
Bring your face to the cerulean surface.
Allow your body to float.

You brought fruit to the river.
What will you bring to the sea?

LETTER TO THE QUEEN OF SWORDS
[Heartland, Iowa City, 1998]

I've been seeing in shapes not in my dreams
but in the air of the day,
geometries of the soul they appear to be.
The love I used to cry for
unfolds its box,

center empty, not even a chair to sit upon.
Without the confine of the box
my arms reach for a sky I knew at birth,
starlight falling, this elsewhere else
I cry for now,

asking What do I seek, no longer asking Who.
Which lineage of shapes did I inherit?
Which can I undo?
Body, can I carry a child?
Body, can I mother?

Which pyramids will appear
in the pupils of my daughter's eyes?
One foot in the present,
one foot in the past,
the Queen of Geometry is asking me

to choose.
Love, let me go until the form I breathe in
forms again, whole and alert,
the patterns of the past obliterated,
cut by the sickle in the sky.

IV

CALIFORNIA II: THE PEACOCK IN THE SPARROW

WHEN WE WERE TWELVE
[Russian River, 1979]

We met in sixth grade, both of us transplants.
You: Ireland. Me: Illinois. We canoed, smoked oregano,
shared a Guinness in my closet. Your parents, mine,

divorcing. Marriage, we agreed, was for fools.
You gave me a red-sleeved shirt, an iron-on sea goat
on the front, a list of Capricorn's better traits on the back —

loyal, confident, hard-working — our birthdays seventeen
days apart. When we were thirteen you asked me to dance,
scratched my initials in the back of your hand with a pin.

At fourteen, you cajoled me into your VW bug but forgot
to push in the clutch; five times we hit the Post Office wall.
Seventeen years later you call. I'm in the heartland

teaching English, you're an Ironman triathlete
tuning bicycles. I think: Freckles, braces, skinny legs.
You invite me to Belize. I say, *Let me sleep on it.*

You visit in dream. Through mist, your muscled shoulders
butterfly stroke across the river. *Come to me*, I say,
turning down Belize. You deplane wearing a black

Navy pea coat, a book of unread Tsvetaeva under your arm.
The blizzard you arrive in persists for a week. We ski
the streets by moonlight, kiss under the constellation

of Orion, call our parents with our news. In my future:
thirteen poems you'll write on our anniversary,
one for each letter in my maiden name.

MORNING SICKNESS

I grip the rail. Slate surf sides the ferry.
Dartwhips of the dolphins of Dunlaughrie

parallel our course. Their even leaps give
an illusion of stillness my body craves.

The cold wind comforts, something to lean
against, numbing nose-tip, lips, throat,

numbing the fact of forward motion.
At this velocity I cannot pretend

that nothing's changed. Inside, at a booth,
my husband sits across from his sister

playing cards. I feel the propeller blades
churn the sea, vibrate the deck, drone home

our difference: I'm the host, forever changed:
he'll remain the same.

BOHEMIAN GROVE

My belly fills the kayak's cockpit,
my sides brush the rims, I float

like the bubble in a spirit level
unable to find plumb. I chase you

up the shallows. The pebbles grate
but do not slow your pace.

Past empty cabins, maroon paint
peeling, porches without screens,

a private property sign chained
to a cliff where you intend to jump.

Twice I call you off. Then your
kayak answers, empty, nudges

mine, then drifts away. You dive.
Adrenaline arcs down both my arms,

through my heart and through
our unborn child. We listen for you;

holding our breath. After, I try
to let it be enough, the palm of silt

you bring me from the bottom, rivuleting
back into the river down your wrist.

COOKIES, OR THE THREE OF SWORDS

I'm not good alone. Wedding band shed,
barefoot in late afternoon,
packed dirt of forest backyard cold on my insteps.

The one time I call her, adrenaline's maypole
spinning in my chest, she doesn't answer.

The counselor we call the Hobbit (short, sincere, timid)
says: *He's still grieving*
over getting his hand slapped
for reaching into the cookie jar without even getting a cookie.

I wish he'd eaten one; I could leave without regret.

Longing's the sin – his for her, mine to possess him –
not who I thought I was.

I leave for ten days so he can decide which cookie he wants.

My best friend takes my three kids –
my reason to leave, my reason to stay.

I imagine life without him.

The Hobbit calls to say my husband's sorry.
I agree to meet.
The Hobbit lists everything good we've said about us.

At Goat Rodeo, nested hearts
fall from the barista's foam wand.
I read it as an omen.

THE MARRIAGE COUNSELOR CHANNELS KING SOLOMON

You have to imagine it, everything halved.
Three children, the husky, the cat.
And everything doubled. Bedrooms, debt, grief.

But didn't imagination bring us here?
Yours: What a stranger could do for you.
Mine: What else did I not know?

What's real are the hours I nursed our babies
in our bed, my sleepless vigilance that neither
of us rolled over on them in our sleep.

What's real are the hours you stayed
in swimmer's reach of them in the river
no matter the current's speed.

Vultures orbit in decelerating circles
above the cliffs where we first met as children,
moon like a coin of trust we must both earn back.

KOLMER GULCH
[Northern California Coast, 2008]

Down the cragged, nettled incline
past two crosses for the drowned,

our children scale pocked rocks.
I'm at forty-nine seconds, scanning

kelp-threaded waves for the black thumb
of your hood. I remember swimming

hand in hand in Fiji, the time-slowed
undulations of sea cucumbers, pale tan,

rolling their octagonal lanterns
across the miniature ribs of the sand.

But this is the cold Pacific, overcast,
zero visibility according to the pair

of retreating divers you passed in the surf.
Our son straddles a feeder stream, flings

strands of algae and one unlucky
minnow into his sister's hair.

You surface. I breathe. Then I lose
you again, as I do daily to their needs:

our youngest is crying, "Up!" Our
son's now lost a shoe. Our daughter

begs to bring her dead minnow home.
I just want you – hurtling crown first

towards the silver lid of the sea
you must open to live – now kicking

in, the three rust-red half-helmets
of abalone suctioned to your chest.

ECLIPSE

*It only takes a few seconds to burn your retina
for life,* I tell my daughter. *You won't even feel it*

while it's happening. I want to add: *just about
as long as it could take for you to get pregnant*

or have a car accident. She's driving the coast
with my husband past Shell Beach today, none of us

in the direct path of the eclipse. My son slipped out
to surf before I could remind him not to look.

I must stop worrying. My husband says I must.
Did you know there are mountaintops in India

surrounded by perpetual layers of mist? On these
sister sky islands live birds of the same species

so long separated since the glaciers retreated,
not only have they forgotten there's life

below the clouds, they've invented songs
the others no longer recognize as their own.

POTATO

It sits in a flimsy pie-tin of crimped and corrugated silver,
wrapped in a paper towel my daughter wets three times
a day. My son tells her to chop it, one eye per chunk,

bury it in the yard, then dig it up. But she's like me,
needs to see it grow. It's an Idaho potato, nothing special,
useful under the right cut of meat in the crockpot.

It withers toward its center, wrinkling a bit like me,
color sucked from my hair's roots by – I don't know –
this – arguing over why potato eyes are called eyes

when they're seeds: *Put down the knife. Leave her
project be.* She's not sure she wants it now. Once
I saw my 12-string guitar in the hands of the mover

my husband hired – *My lucky day*, he said and smiled.
My husband right behind: *She never plays it, take it away.*
What did he know of the grad school hours, how

it saved me from myself? Useless now in a house
of crying babies. I see, with my blind potato eyes I see,
and for days I dream guitars washing up, like parts of me.

DROPPING IN THE EIGHT

Back wheels propped against vertical wall,
board hanging free out over the bowl –
one foot on, one foot off – three times

my ten-year-old son hesitates, looks up
to make sure I'm watching through the chain link
fence. It kicks up a panic in me like walking

under blimps or swimming in open sea.
When I nod, glance away in respect,
he commits, vanishes below the concrete lip

to the decisive click of his front wheels' contact
and the silver rhythmic scroll of his arc. I listen
for his proportion of momentum: what he gathers

on descent must propel him out onto the far rim.
Practice doesn't help: the fear never goes,
he tells me, no matter how many times

you drop in. The thirty-somethings behind
the skate park's desk agree, ringing up Gatorade
for sweaty dollars they push upside down

and wrinkled into the plastic cash register
between coaching newbies and spraying
disinfectant into helmets. My son undoes

his chin strap, dirt and sweat streaking cheeks,
knee and elbow scabbed with yesterday's
dozen attempts to clear the cone and grab

the edge of board with one hand to stick
the landing, his thumb a mottled salmon red
sanded and bleeding into his grip tape.

KEY

    Hiding from my daughter in the garage,
    I lean into my husband's arms, washing
    machine at my back.

    She's done nothing
    but claim a boy across the street to love
    on her thirteenth birthday.

    Her body is the key
    that opens the door behind which lie
    my girlhood selves.

    At fourteen I was raped.

    This is the threshold I couldn't foresee.

    Why can't I, I think —
    like every other mother —
    slide back in time into our Briar Rose hours,

    one hundred years
    of respite in which to dream.

    How can I raise a daughter?

OPOSSUM

Two bare-thighed female boxers face off
on an LA billboard in the persimmon dusk,
gloves poised over twelve lanes of traffic,

eyebrows manicured, French braids wet, lips
glossed like lovers, beautiful Goliaths
my daughter watches pass over us. A kick-boxer,

she dreams of competing in the ring. I think back
to college, self-defense class years after the date rape
when therapy fell short. How Black Belt Kara

insisted when my arms shook under the shame
of women watching me spar, *You can do this.*
She gripped my wrist, said, *If a man is willing*

to grab you off main street in broad daylight,
don't wait to see what he'll do next when he's
dragged you into the alley. But there was no alley

and I played dead. Spines of the floodlights
plank the billboard to lattice our faces in the rear view
mirror – Oh Kara, what happened to our gains?

My daughter's face is placid. I don't know what she sees.
Ten years ago at the neighborhood potluck, the hostess,
after a bottle of wine, brought out her animal cards.

I pulled Opossum. Why? Why not Hawk, even Hare?
I felt ashamed. But now I see it: playing dead
saved my life.

Streetlights of the past wink out. In my own night's
darkness, I coax her from under the lightless shrubs—
filthy, matted with blood and spit, teeth-bared and hissing.

CHOCOLATE ROSE

The rose: everywhere but on the plate.
My son, thirteen, in tears – the concert
where he plans to present it only an hour

from now. He stands shirtless, barefoot –
brow, chest, and heels black with cocoa,
every drawer, kitchen floor, powdered,

last night's second botched batch
a glistening mass refusing to roll into
its promised sheet. I'm late for work,

his little brother down with the flu,
his sister begging for a ride. I search
for nearby stores that sell premade chocolate

plastic, settle for a recipe he won't need
to chill overnight, de-lid a third can of cocoa,
separate yolk from egg, add one tablespoon

of cold water, not two. It rolls! The petals
hold shape, adhere, warmed by his thumbs!
I pack his rose on ice, drop him in the parking lot

out of view. Ten scant minutes, he's back.
It was perfect! he exults. *I knew she'd love it,*
I say. *No...she'll open it later,* he smiles,

delight unmet, unmarred – like mine I hide, to earn
his company. *I handed it to her and vanished –*
he halves the air between us like Houdini.

DAUGHTER BY CANDLELIGHT

She lights a candle in her room.
It means she's staying in: The friends
have lost their grip, she prefers this womb

of pumpkin spice, boyfriend and Circe's loom
an afterthought. She's ours. She bends
to light a candle in her room.

Let her revel in her ample boredom.
Her cat licks amber fur, then wends
to perch on shelf like an heirloom,

glowers at my girl who glares back from
under torn sweatshirt hood she refuses to mend.
She lights another candle in her room.

Discarded on the floor, her shirts' perfume
I gather close to my throat, pretend
our moods, no longer twinned through womb,

do not repel us, volatile with need and blame –
a stage we'll birth from, end nested in beginning, finite bond
I'll grieve by lighting a candle in my room.
Her heartbeat, even in utero, was audible outside my womb.

FULL MOON GHAZAL

The fisherman in the moon drops his net,
diamonds the black sea with his silver net.

Gaps as beautiful as threads in this kind of light,
we'll always swim closer to his widening net.

Look again: no man, only moon, just undines,
the alms of their silver palms forming a net.

None of us know what we want to catch, love
best the hour of possibility: The empty net.

What to do with what we've caught, but heft,
halve, and descale all that glitters in our net.

In my heart all my grunions twist left, then right,
flee – as I, Tania, wish I could flee love's net.

SPELL

I'm a happy mother, she sees that,
Luna, in my lap blocking my pencil's path

to the page. But she also knows I'm no
easy Dorothy ferried by tornado,

knows I wear my Scarlet Letters
for the ways I've said yes, yes,

and yes. *Look at me*, she preens, leans
to dot my chin with cold wet nose,

her paired coronas obelisks that slim to slits
in the sunlight, judge and jury of my hours.

Once, she was all kitten, asleep,
a furled fiddlehead in an abalone shell.

When I truffle my fingers
through her belly's fur, I see it too:

Once I was all girl – for years all mother –
but with Luna, neither.

CHIRON RETURN

On my birth chart the astrologer
marks days when *Chiron goes direct*.
He's your wounded healer,

she explains, *your personal Centaur.*
Most firstborns merge, unaware,
with their mothers. But I know

we're talking about my Sagittarian father.
I hide the papers in my desk, breathe best
inside the weighted vest I wear when I walk

beside the bay. A poison arrow hit its target
when I was two, my brother, one, when
Haight Ashbury acid triggered his manic

depression's undiagnosed oscillations.
After, we lived in consecutive houses
where client's pianos anchored us

with soundboards, each pegged string
under pounds of tension my father
spooled tight to yield perfect pitch.

Can we not return the iron plate
to the forge, start over? Take from him
his quiver, our mother long gone,

our calves reddening in the setting sun?
He's manic again and I, grown daughter,
can no longer ignore this truth –

my children stepping
out of the woods onto the field
directly in our line of sight.

BIRTHMARK

I. San Diego, California

Traversing the tombolo,
the husky pulls leash taut,
bulrush of her pale tail

bobbing. Wind fractures
moonlight on the black bay
into silver hieroglyphics

that rivet my son's stare,
an incantation of light I fear
will pull him out through

the birthmark on my chest
to a home in the ethers
between sea and sun.

II: After the Commune Leader's Exile

When I was my son's age
my uncle visited so briefly
we passed for Normal.

A photographer, he gifted us
one framed image of a Mallard,
Egyptian green arched neck

the color of Mr. Gardner's pond
stippled with cattails – furred tips
so doe-nose damp I couldn't refrain

from tearing the mallow free
to wreathe my shins. What force
it took, denuding each wand!

Remorse immediate. In my dream,
the downy stars circle, rebind,
black roots facing out, cinched

to form a velvet hull. Then London,
a rainwet brick-ribbed street, sooty
face of the lamplighter, pole

forced through my heart. Once
I believed with our Leader that I too
fell to Earth pure, I too was Chosen.

The scar follows me, this body,
this life, coin below my collarbone
tallow gold – debt paid, son mine.

STRENGTH: TAROT'S ARCANUM VIII

Undone, I'm the girl in the gown
holding the jaw of the lion,
his breath at my crotch. Or perhaps

my daughter wears the gown
and I wear the mane. I know no lion
nor girl that mimic this pair,

benign, garland-crowned, sated,
though once when I was ten
I wrestled my mother's will and won.

I stood on a chair with a hammer
to curtain in the outdoor cat
who sneaked in to birth her litter

in the attic sewing room, where
I'd tried on my mother's wedding dress
in secret, my body – near breastless –

larger than hers at nineteen, when
pregnant with me, she married
my father. When the zipper caught

at my rib's base, I didn't force it,
nor did she insist I chase the cat
away. I was larger than she and alone

in the room. Four sheer black sacs
shimmer loose as the cat spins, mews,
tears the kittens free: first paws,

then V's of ears, the frail gray
milkweed pods of their eyes seamed
shut despite the heat of her tongue.

THE DAUGHTERS OF STELLE
[California, Summer 2017]

— *"There was no guessing his kith or kin,"* Robert Browning

In the fairytale, the Pied Piper's flute is magic.
Lured to the Corn by your words, what our parents

couldn't know — even after they decreed you
a fraud — was how far into the mountain's

portal the Chosen Children followed.
The years it might take us to come back.

I hear you died in prison, cancer of the throat.
I marvel at the incantatory power of your book,

I wonder, Does what comes through the flute
bend the will of the player?

In my father's house today: a cutting board singed
with letters that spell the name *Stelle* —

the town you created for us, where we'd learn to live
in community, apart from the farmers around us.

I know how to see the peacock in the sparrow —
I was born with that, can't blame you.

I know the terrain — as once on a cigarette-stained
Greyhound bus I received news, by cellphone,

of my mother's cancer. Through the trapezoid
glass, silver ladders of the harbor cranes

failed to reach the clouds
though they doubled beneath the sea.

FORTNITE WIDOW

Dinner's ready, come to the table when you die.
It's my refrain, back home after two weeks

of caring for my mother. I've lost my sons,
my husband too. He calls himself The Medic.

Six-year-olds from England, Canada, New York
ask, *Are you a boy or a girl?* A fair question –

his avatar's a muscular female who wears
black and white camouflage, a pink backpack,

her hair in a ponytail. He stations our two couches
in rows like airplane seats, buys a second screen,

gold controllers. He sits behind my sons
and shouts Navy SEAL tactical orders. They play

worse when he watches. I tell him, *You can't
give advice unless you learn to play.* A mistake.

He does just that. Doles out Band-Aids to the wounded,
swears when knocked by snipers or pick-axed to death,

Why can't they just leave me crawling? Most often
taken out by the storm, lamenting the treasure he'll forfeit,

as the cone of light descends to claim his Medic's soul,
his meatloaf under plastic wrap cooling on the counter.

V

CALIFORNIA III: BERKELEY POSTCARD

BERKELEY POSTCARD
[Berkeley, California, 2017]

During the hour I took away from our mother's dying
to hike Claremont Canyon and back, the postcard
pasted itself to the bench in the rain. Black

ballpoint ink, a signed work, a girl with long
black hair in a galaxy cloak with two unslippered
toes edging the horizon line, a pocked planet's

porthole overhead. On the reverse, crosshatched,
the Milky Way: definite planets, spokes of stars —
as if through my mother's eyes — this paper door,

my brother asleep beside his wife on one side
and my fear of the dark on the other, rain on the roof
and the indifferent silver in-breath of BART taking

our mother night by night from us, her breathing
the only inside-the-house sound we listened for,
her face to the wall, mouth open, the tip of her nose

ashening, ash blue as if tipped in snow, the midnight
hospice nurse unalarmed, unmoved, like the artist—
did he mean to leave his girl out in the rain?

How I needed her, expressionless face drying
under my brother's lamp and slid into a plastic sleeve,
closed between pages of my notebook to keep.

CITY OF METAPHORS: SIX MONTHS LATER

So quickly by car we drove into Berkeley
in reverse order from the way we walked it
in the growing span of hours mother slept. Here

the pale plywood cutouts in front of a house just
past the Claremont Hotel: A woman in hat bent
at waist, her watering can, her silhouette

offspring — two children — all three holding
hands, metaphor for her disappearing. Here
the intersection, the light, the crosswalk,

Casa de Chocolat, truffles she'll never buy
sweating in their counter set back from the front
window sun, here Timeless Coffee where she ate

her last bite of chocolate cake, here the rose bush
she loved, blooming for every anonymous walker.
Here the doorway, threshold's gap, where undertaker's

gurney dropped to the sidewalk, cream roses
of the hospice nurse's bouquet and pink peonies
we picked and de-petalled to circle her body, crushed

close now and staining up through my sister-in-law's
white cotton sheet. All night my little sister
binge watches *Black Mirror*, then *Dark Matter*,

in which the beautiful convicts and assassins wake,
memory erased, willing to love again,
orphaned over and over in the same incarnation.

ATRIUM

They're here for people like us —
those two-foot metal origami birds

strung on wires that zag the hospital's
atrium sky from floors 2 to 6

blue   green   red   yellow
like some primary color zoo meant

to calm the tantrum we cannot
have. We sit on the cool slats

of a fake wood bench. Century ferns
arch their pharaoh fans to cove us

in false harbor. Who did the math?
Weight of bird, suspension's tension,

force of gravity, rust by rain —
at what point will rivets fail,

how long will those lines hold
those birds in their staggered flight?

CHAPEL

A basket of pastel paper leaves,
a hell of an Eden — go ahead,

bring spring to the tree, its dead
trunk moored in a bucket

of rocks. I finally admitted
to a friend — from the 10th floor

overlooking the atrium, origami
metal birds bisected by supporting

wires and diagonally lit where
the late morning sun meets

the hospital's shadow — I get it.
It's time. To give her back to God.

As if the choice were mine. I write
my life's worth of thanks, find

an empty branch on which to hang
my leaf, where it turns obstinately

sideways and take two prayer
pamphlets instead of *One per family.*

SANCTUARY

After the commune, she raised us
churchless, and since then,
her new religion is not mine —

does it matter what any of us believe —
there's no definition of God that losing her
to cancer fits. Respect the migraine

that burgeons when she offers
her church's book with its directions
for how to soothe her. Accept

those same directions spoken,
by her, in her voice: How to calm her
in the patterns of calming familiar to her.

Put your palm to her heart — she's afraid.
When she says, "I don't wish to be a burden"
say, "Remember, I'm a mother too."

Stay until she falls asleep. Mend
the spiritual dissonance in your gut
afterwards, alone, at a church

of neither faith — not hers, not yours —
a pure metaphor for house that houses
stranded souls. It stands on the main street

on a slight sloped lawn, Celtic
stained-glass mandala lit, a stone path
that ends in a stone bench beneath a pair

of flowering plum trees that shelter
the view of the rush hour walkers
and the auroras of sorrow that follow.

SISTERS, OR WALDO PUDDING

It starts at the house when we hug
the dog walker stumbling into the doorframe,

so kind he matches our manic grip,
his massive hoop of keys against our hips,

the tangible promise of hours of dogs to walk
on the other side of this moment

we can no longer bear. It's not that we
Let Go or *Accept* nor that we back off

our vigilant care to keep our mother
from falling or wanting, it's just that

the bakery case's interior lemony light lures
us to bend to scrutinize each tier of velvet

frosted confections, pastel confetti coined
and frilled in violet cuplets, pale green

marzipan cloaked cakes parked on scalloped
under-sheets. We stalk a beautiful woman

down the bread, pasta, and organic make-up
aisles, her indigo gold eye shadow, her silk lapels,

white lace stockings disappearing into red
and black leather cowboy boots.

We tell the checkout girl when she asks
Having a good day? the truth about the nurses

of hospice: *they're angels, all — don't refuse them,*
that this little Waldo pudding (our name for it)

in its tiny shot glass hat   white   tan   white
will be our mother's last dessert.

DUCK

Everything that is black is healthy.
Everything that is white is not.
He won't say cancer even though

he's read her chart: Chemo,
clearly cancer, two years ago.
He taps her x-ray: Everywhere, snow—

throat, lungs, torso — fistfuls of snow,
circle after circle, obscuring her spine.
We have a saying, he says (he's a cliché:

fit, young, kind) *that if it looks like a duck*
and it quacks like a duck, it's probably
a duck. My brother beside my mother

on the crinkling white paper. We know,
she knows, the duck knows. Miffy knows,
my first bunny, I mean book, *Miffy*

in the Snow. With an x for a mouth,
red mittens, matching scarf, a red hat
in the exact shape of her ears that matches

her boots, yellow skates, a thin blue strip
of lake, the blue in its lane, her hat
on her ears, the snow on the ground.

DEATH COCOON: SISTER-IN-LAW
—For Maria

Akin to envy, that feeling, watching her leave:
Out at 8, back at 5, mail in one hand, a paper sack
with my mother's prescriptions in the other,
a cloth net bag sagging with each night's savory,

the way, even here, at home, she closes the kitchen door,
leaving us, already too long with ourselves, again.
From under the door's gap, mint, rosemary,
the sound of cuts of meat caramelizing in one of her pans,

her casual culinary skill, and the way she says
Want to read this, I'm done with it, you might like it,
along with the loan of her library card, *Smoke*
Gets in Your Eyes and Other Lessons from the Crematory,

her perfect Red Riding Hood lipstick, black glasses
framing her brown eyes and when the wolf comes for me,
the way she puts her warm knitter's hands
over mine while I cry.

LOOK, WE SAY, LOOK

Look — the first command —
lilac, sunflower, little bee —

first hand holding yours.
First sound — voice of mother,

You are here, world bordered
by her witness: *Look.*

She's half awake, half asleep
in her blue hat, blue mittens,

blue knit shoes, neck tilted back
as we pass hedges of rosemary

she used to crush between her fingers.
November's trees rocket red

and siren gold, burning into Berkeley's
wan blue no cloud sky.

Look Mama, I say, *Look* —
her wheelchair crossing the gaps

that delineate each square
of sidewalk in even increments,

click, click, click — like tiny garden
gates closing beneath us.

TAROT READING, MORNING BEFORE

No Death card falls, just the Tower,
with its promise of hurtling headfirst
without my mother, barefoot, crownless,

to the ground, God's lightning spiking
my spine. Respite: Miss Fisher's Murder
Mysteries, back-to-back episodes,

countdown on the screen: 4, 3, 2, 1…
Phryne at the wheel of her white
convertible, in her exquisite frock

and pumps, black hair fringing
the curve of her chin, her forever crush
on married detective Jack, drinks

in their hands in front of her fireplace.
After, I rest, lights out, on the couch.
Paddles of my mother's wheelchair

face in and flare, as if sparking,
parked outside her door, door ajar.
Listen to the pace — slight — quickening —

her breath — as it mingles with Eden's
velvet hedge in the dream
of a stranger I did not invite, his peach

parachute settling over us. Damp strips
of his skin — swaths of shoulder, then
thighs — peel up out of my palms

as he falls, spiraling through me
in even rings I cannot halt, appalled,
undone, barefoot, waking alone.

BUDDHA BOARD
—For Natasha Marie

If we were true Buddhas, we'd let them fade —
our turns at the board — wetting the slate
parked over a narrow trough of water.

Comes with a brush, your palette restricted
to a spectrum of blacks, grays, and the final white
of evaporating strokes. But instead

we photograph our paintings as they ghost,
like this one: a child holding a kite,
her string the first thing to vanish.

VISITORS

She didn't want any visitors, barely us,
her three children, but what were we to say,
reluctant midwives of her remaining minutes,

writing down like a list of birth contractions
the number of her breaths per minute
her final hours. But this came early,

in the luxury of weeks, the day after
Halloween, when the doctor promised
she'd make it to Christmas

and left us waiting for two weeks
to see the palliative care team
which would only refer her to hospice.

Five trips to ER for meds to control
the pain that caused her nausea —
which created more pain — she

in her forever pajamas with red cardinals,
wanting only to sleep, and when awake,
to watch *Great British Bake Off*

where it rains perpetually onto the great
white tent, hallucinatory wet greens
and purples of the garden surrounding

the neat rows of bakers tending their ovens,
praying their challenge cakes rise
each crying when they won.

DIANA, PRINCESS OF THE AMAZONS
[Wonder Woman, 2017, Patty Jenkins, Director]

Home from ER, we waste no time:
I prop our mother up, tuck the green O
of the empty vomit sock below the futon.

My sister opens her laptop and there she is,
Gal Gadot, running up the stronghold's wall
in her ash-blue skirt, bodice copper red,

third eye star-crowned, Lasso of Hestia
volcanic orange and ashimmer over
her lover-boy spy's torso. Gal improvises

lines that make our mother, twice-divorced,
loverless, laugh: "Men are essential for procreation,
but when it comes to pleasure, unnecessary."

Is there any bullet she cannot stop,
wrist/wrist/spin — slow-motion frames
we've craved for years, the three of us

shoulder to shoulder until the credits roll,
the pain returns,
and we pack again for the ER.

BUDDHA HINDSIGHT

In the mother daughter dark
in the selfish hours

before the hospice single bed arrives
I lie beside her on the futon.

She listens. My kids, my husband.
Her turn: *Maybe I shouldn't have left your father.*

I hold my breath. She rolls on her side to look at me.
I keep my eyes on the ceiling,

> her kindergarten yellow shape sorter's box upside
> down, door
>
> > open
> >
> > circle
> >
> > square
> >
> > star
> >
> > crescent moon
> >
> > falling beside him,
> > beside Brush and Hush
> > the Color Kittens
>
> from the land where "Red Is Red
> And Blue is Blue."

She answers before I can form the question.

I know we fought a lot. Ran around on each other....
I could've tried harder.

But no regrets about the commune.
If you never leave what you know,
how can you grow?

BIRTHDAY
—For Gabriella

"Isn't it fitting that on his birthday I decide" —
she means her decision to order death meds
on my husband's birthday. I push her towards

the roses where she'll name the one we've seen for days,
wide petalled velvet and Godiva red, after her hospice
nurse Gabriella. "He loves life so much,

always in motion." "Yes," I reply, then start to cry
behind her. My husband, the triathlete, is waking up
alone today with our children.

"Let's go buy a card," she adds. I think she means
for him, but she means for Gabriella.
At the flower stand, she picks a pink fairy hovering

and sprinkling stars over a baby buggy,
the kind of card you buy for a new mother.
"That's Gabriella, raining down her stars, waving

her wand over me." Then she selects one manicured
rose, petals tight, pristine and pruned, so unlike
the Godiva we left living on its stem.

We leave what she writes on the card, knowing
what she meant — swell, special, quintessential —
you are so very squella, Gabriella.

EIGHT OF SWORDS

I've decided, I'm done, she says to Gabriella —
to us — but her body isn't, like the girl, gowned

in vital red, arms bound, blindfold grey under
a sky of grey, the ineffectual swords of mind

lined up at her side. It rained that day
and by next morning she would be gone.

I had no question for the Tarot cards,
but they spoke to me like old friends:

She needs you, daughter, I didn't even care
if it was simply what I wanted to hear.

She was no longer speaking, neither awake
nor in a coma, all of us on this side of

one more night together
in which to dream — she too —

so we listened to the light rain, the artist
not yet having misplaced his postcard

on the bench for me to find with its forecast,
her next step:

blindfold removed, arms unbound, feet bare,
roof below her

haloed circles of planets
and stars closer,

some part of me unable
to stop following —

Look, Mama, Look.

CLOSET

She calls us to her room
to divide her clothes between us
our hands damp as they meet

over each silk shirt
as we protest, *No, polka dots
look best on you. This green's*

so you — your hazel eyes!
Three times she says,
"I want to keep that —"

we bend quick to find a hanger,
press our brother's arrow quivers
and dress pants aside,

secure a spot in the very back
for her wool winter jacket
and one white eyelet blouse and skirt,

she in her pjs with red cardinals
like any other mother on a Tuesday
watching her daughters sift, sort,

and spin
without argument
in front of her mirror.

CLAREMONT CANYON HIKE

I kiss my mother on the forehead
each time I leave. Firm, angry the kiss:

Be here when I get back. Across hills,
power lines power my brother's city;

cables suspend bridges. Closer in,
on the nearest tree a rope waits for a leaper

as panting dogs and sunset hikers
pass; a professor explains the proper

placement of the semi-colon. I stand
on the sheared eucalyptus trunk, its grey

growth rings sun-warped and cracked apart
in the center, a dark star under my legs —

a portal, an air stem, like the one they say
anchors our spirit to our body when we travel

in dream on the astral. I peer down, unable
to see the decayed roots meet the soil.

EMPEROR OF TRANSPORT

At 5 am he walks me out — sweet emperor
of transport — my brother, in his robe,

the peonies on the shrub pinker in the rain.
My mother in her wheelchair at the table

waits for him to heat her soup — my job — I must
trust him to it. I've been trying not to cry

but crying won and wins, all the ride.
A naked Barbie on the floor behind the Uber

driver's seat, all the city streets so quickly passed
where mincingly my mother walked,

the same set of blocks we drove to and from ER.
There's the tenth floor, top of Kaiser,

I can see her middle room. Her next stay,
that corner suite where we watched a full moon

rise over the bridge, and the see-through curtains
drop at dusk — my sister and brother and I

sleeping in shifts on the burgundy window-seat.
My driver asks, *How are you*, and I manage,

It's my mother, she's real sick. She apologizes
for the Barbie — it belongs to her kid.

That's where I'm headed now, home to my three
children, trying to forget my mother's voice, hug,

how she asked, *But when are you coming back?*
Every freeway brake-light a blood bead.

TWO GARDENS

When I wake from the dream of sleeping
with Death, her breathing speeds. I rise
and sit by her side; she's at 20 breaths

per minute now. There's nothing left
to do. I've written down one more Kahlil
Gibran quote, *Sadness is but a wall between*

two gardens, one of those *We think you'll
like this* emails, 6:25 a.m., from Pinterest.
I've watched the slideshow looping in its

frame on her bedside table by the silver bell
she'd ring when she needed us: Here she stands
on graduation day with her father, here,

six years old, reaching her arm into a silver pot,
here at two in her toddler's daffodil dress.
6:51, I write, 21 breaths per minute, paint

a tree trunk on the Buddha Board with parallel
branches, give up on the leaves. Paint,
then dislike, one childish heart that floats

then fades beside the tree. At 7:00, 22 breaths
per minute, it's time to wake my brother and sister.
By 7:33 she's in the second garden.

THE KNIGHT OF SWORDS AND THE SIBLING TREE

The Knight fell in the position "The Unconscious."
Like me, the Fool — firstborn daughter:
I'd rush in, fix it. But I was one of three birds,

bridge swallows, far below, without a bridge,
the horse of God above. In the saddle God
with dragonfly wings stenciled with letters

West   East   South   North
spinning so fast you could read each word
as the horse sped onward. We spun too,

mother's last breath two minutes behind us,
the three of us turning to make a trunk,
arms linked across shoulders, heads bowed.

We breathed in that stale pale star of air
between our bodies, Buddha Board beside her
returning to its milk-sky mirror state.

TREE SYNCHRONICITY
   —*For Barbara Ann*

    I wish it were a labyrinth but it is an archer's
   target on the journal's cover, made of Kapukapu
   and waru leaves, three circles of descending

    size, red leaf pressed over green, each ring,
   even the bullseye, bordered in thin rolled cord.
   We're in my friend's kitchen, she's sprung me

    of my brother's house, took my mother's hands
   in hers and promised to bring me back soon.
   Death is stronger than chocolate, I tell her,

    but she's a writer, knows to hand me this fair-trade
   blank journal and a tin of tea, "Ancient Trees,"
   each musty coin inside wrapped in paper you remove

    before you steep. Weeks after all this is over, when
   my brother brings me a box of our mother's things —
   woolen coat, eyelet shirt and skirt — I make a cup

    of Tree Tea, open the journal with its saffron pages,
   scent of turmeric, choose a pen, drop below soil line
   to the roots and begin again.

NORWEGIAN AIR

I'm a mother who just lost her mother,
afraid to raise my arm, to make a mistake.

I'd like a headset too, call button close
but I refrain, watch the shadows cast by the watchers

ear-phoned to their tiny screens in the blue false dusk
the floor-light silts over my shins.

From LA to Copenhagen the sleepers sleep.
Three days before she died she stopped talking.

Someone I love asked me if I'd asked her
all my questions. They meant well.

It's been thirty years since I've seen the mermaid.
I was eighteen.

How small she seemed, floating alone in the harbor,
her breasts below the waterline.

This time the tide is out. Snow clings to her base.
I can walk up, touch her if I wish, this arrested

version: this free girl before she followed
an alien boy to shore.

I'm thinking of my daughter, seventeen, all
the hours left to raise her. Daughter-trouble

in every mother's future, the only cure
the sound of your own mother's voice reeling

you back from whatever state of deprivation
you decided to suffer:

Hello, Hello honey, What's up, buttercup.
She knew it was you before she picked up.

MIRAGE
[Coronado, California, 2019]

Summer's end, we stall
by walking. Our ritual, our husky
pulling. Hours away in his late

afternoon my father at his bench
stalls Parkinson's by playing
the same Bela Bartok I love

that he learned when he was twenty,
the sharps and flats as fleeting
as the bike path minnows

of the baby lizards at our feet
that vanish into the bay silt.
A hotel taxi with its open car fringed

in blue beeps as it passes, portly
parents in row seats. Their sullen
boys face us as they recede

and stare unchecked, their plastic
buckets full of broken sea stars.
I am sorry for the hours I wished

I were someone else's child, late
for curfew, grounded, ashamed
of our poverty. I wish

I were listening in your house
beneath the painting of the moon,
sculpture of kestrel made of spoons

spinning, the cat thin as a sock
that adopted you
mowling to be let in.

NOCTILUCA

    Bless the peacock's fan of astral eyes,
    wolf's winter face spoked and furred

    at timberline, the fallopian oboe
    of the whale sonorous with grief

    unrelinquished. In dream
    you are the hidden thing, rescued

    by sonar of song, edges of your body
    hazeled, silvering from crown

    to shoulders, arms too, view of hands
    prolonging the lucid dream's

    brief escape from self as a girl
    barefoot on chilled wet ground

    in hip high grass, ranks of fireflies
    shedding haloes the quarter mile

    to the farmhouse. No one waits up
    but the porch light is on, bare bulb

    clotted with insects bearing wings
    hematite laced and Hades green.

LETTER TO THE EIGHT-YEAR-OLD LIVING IN THE CORN

You still read Nancy Drew, framed by upstairs farmhouse window, where dusk begins at noon and snow blurs the trees at cornfield's edge. If mother were home, you'd help her cut red velvet for your Christmas dress, your legs on top of hers on the stool in front of the attic sewing machine as the iron treadle rocks and needle grazes fingers to stitch fast the invisible zipper.

But the house is empty except for the snap of mousetrap and the thud of rabbit a hawk lost to the roof — or you, falling out of bed. She's waitressing in town or on the lap of a farmer's son. Father quarters cows at the butcher shop with his piano man's hands.

Back to *The Secret of the Old Clock* and Nancy: ever happy, ever able. At eight, you were old enough to want red high heels, not old enough to know why. By 38, you'll guess it was less the shoes, more the purpose — a purpose larger than to land a lover: a mystery to solve, thief to catch, Fool self to forgive. Beginning, middle, end — tidy comfort against approaching car-lights beveling the night-dank windows and pupils of a waiting child.

Back to the midnight acre of corn — I've come for you — smiling, remembering how you played piano in the basement without a lamp to practice for your first recital:

if you can play alone in the dark by heart
you'll find your way in the light
with a hundred strangers
staring at your back.

GRATITUDES:

Thank you to my late mother, Mary, for the hours you cared for me and sewed my clothes, for your strength, spunk, and humor. For your ability to see the good and to persevere. We miss you.

To my father, thank you for inspiring my love of poetry and music, for the bravest of pattern-breaking, for the desire to take us to a place that supported ideals of "peace and love," and for sharing with me that Stelle did "deliver on its promise of kindred spirits" with "so many idealistic, earnest people."

To Ruth Thompson: for the doors you open, for the heart-walk through this life, and for expecting nothing less than rigorous mining for soul gold. You are a delight.

To Don Mitchell: for your devotion to bringing every book into most excellent form; I thank you with all my heart.

To Nancee: for reflecting back to me that one of the ways the mothers of Stelle gauged the community's success was to ask, in hindsight, how the children fared as they grew up and went out into the world past Stelle's borders. Thank you for your generous reflection: "You are thriving, raising children, writing poetry; look at the gifts."

To Stephen: for your music and the formative journaling exercises based on our class's nature walks and those based on imaginary journeys.

To Ava: for your embodiment of joy, beauty, and play. As our babysitter and friend, you brought color, music, and laughter.

To David: for the depth of your kindness and the heart-to-hearts we had when you took care of us.

To Sandy: for your warmth and love and the way you placed me under your wing when it mattered most and cared for me as one of your daughters.

To Jamila: for the photos of us as children at Stelle and your joy, innocence, and enthusiasm that helped me strive to point these poems sunward in revision.

To Gloria Smit: for reconnecting so kindly and sharing your writing about Stelle.

To my godfather Uncle Joe: for a lifetime of your beautiful photographs that showed me at an early age the magic of kinship with nature.

To Duane: for understanding commune and cult dynamics and for supporting my journey in poems, and as a person, always.

To Donna Agins: for your boundless generosity and spiritual wisdom regarding the layers of revision and the soul care that needs to accompany them; I couldn't have finished this book without you.

To Sandra Coomer: for reaching into my life one spring over the phone and taking up residence in my heart ever after. Thank you for the gift of the Rockvale Review, Rockvale Writers' Colony, and your own poetry.

To Katie Manning: for the gift of Whale Road Review, your beautiful poetry, and for your support.

To Barbara Rockman: for your passion, fearlessness in your own poetry, and depth of witnessing.

To the Feisty Writers Tribe: Marni Freedman, memoir teacher, treasured friend and more for helping me believe. Nicola Ranson for early vital feedback and kindred insight. Phyllis Erickson, Kimberly Joy, Jen Laffler, Lindsey Salatka, Gina Simmons Schneider, Suzanne Spector, Barbara Thomson, Nancy Villalobos and Anastasia Zadeik for astute guidance during revision.

To the Flamingos: Jayne Benjulian for fierce and loving exacting editorial winnowing; Lisa Rizzo and Barbara Yoder for holding me accountable to the manuscript's best incarnation. For holding the vision for over a decade: Sandra Hunter, Marcia Meier, and Michel Wing.

To Janeen: for your compassionate passion, loving mirror, and for always being in my corner.

To Rachel Pollack: for your tarot inspiration and permission to use the quote from *Seventy-Eight Degrees of Wisdom* (1980).

To my husband Mark and our three children, Kalli, Orion, and Nik: for the gift of our family heart, our timeless hours walking with Sisu by the sea at Goat Rock, and a lifetime of joy.

To my heart tribe: Mary Allen, Vilma Baumann, Robyn Beattie, Elizabeth Brennan, Sandy Frank, Patricia Hall, Kathleen Meyer, Corinne Stanley, Lydia Stewart, Penina Taesali, and Jerilynn Wagner.

Last and most especially, to Michelle, Leslie, Elizabeth Ann, and Molly: my love and gratitude for the childhood Illinois hours we shared.

ENDNOTES

THE ULTIMATE FRONTIER: Describes the physical cover of the book, *The Ultimate Frontier*, published by The Stelle Group (1963) and authored by Richard Kieninger, pen name Eklal Keushana (translation: Fountainhead of Christ). Cover art depicts three of Kieninger's alleged prior incarnations.

CHOSEN: Lemuria was an ancient land inhabited by a peace-loving civilization that purportedly existed and disappeared beneath the sea due to cataclysmic event or pole shift.

FRONTIER II: PORTRAIT: *The Education of Oversoul Seven* (one of the Seth Books, written by the channel Jane Roberts) was originally published in 1979.

COUCH BURNING: *The Left Hand of Darkness* by Ursula K. Le Guin (1969).

MOSCOW ROAD: *Life after Life* was written by Raymond Moody (1975).

THE PAGE OF WANDS AT THE WELLNESS FAIR: The tarot card referenced is from the Aquarian Tarot deck by David Palladini (1986).

POETRY RULES IN THE HEARTLAND: Cites the poetry collection *August Zero* by Jane Miller (1993).

BLACK'S GASLIGHT VILLAGE: The tarot card referenced is from the Rider Waite Smith deck (1909).

SNOWFLAKE BENTLEY: *Snow Crystals* was written by Wilson A Bentley (1931). The Köln Concert, solo piano improvisation performance by Keith Jarrett, was recorded on January 24, 1975 at the Opera House in Cologne.

TRADING READINGS: The sample deck referred to is The Beasts of Albion illustrated and created by Miranda Gray (1994).

Hall Mall: Iowa City: The White Brotherhood, a group of non-carnate advisors the Leader refers to in *The Ultimate Frontier* who were purported to direct humanity's lessons towards greater evolvement and higher consciousness.

Opossum: The opossum card referenced is from the Medicine Cards deck by Jamie Sams and David Carson (1988).

Key: Briar Rose: After the fairytale by Brothers Grimm, Little Briar Rose.

Eclipse: National Geographic documents this occurrence of birds and sky islands in "Breathtaking Sky Islands Showcase Evolution in Action" by Shaena Montanari (2017).

Chiron Return: An astrological term; Chiron, the smallest planet in solar system, appears in one's birth chart and "returns" usually just once (roughly 49-50 years after birth) often associated with a chance to heal unresolved wounds. In Greek mythology, Chiron is a Centaur, known for his knowledge of medicine and his wisdom, also referred to as the "wounded healer."

Strength: "Tarot's Arcanum VIII": The tarot card referenced is from the Rider Waite Smith deck (1909).

Daughters of Stelle: References Robert Browning's poem, "Pied Piper of Hamelin" (1842).

Sisters, or Waldo Pudding: *Where's Waldo?* by Martin Hanford (1987).

Duck: *Miffy in the Snow* by Dick Bruna and Patricia Crampton (1963).

Death Cocoon: Sister-in-law: *Smoke Gets in Your Eyes and Other Lessons from the Crematory* by Caitlin Doughty (2014).

Tarot Reading Morning Before: "Eight of Swords," "Emperor of Transport," and "Knight of Swords and The Sibling Tree" reference tarot cards from the Rider Waite Smith deck (1909).

Diana: Princess of the Amazons: "One of Wonder Woman's best scenes was entirely improvised" by Julia Alexander, Polygon; see polygon.com/2017/6/9/15772134/wonder-woman-improv

Buddha Hindsight: *The Color Kittens* by Margaret Wise Brown (1949).

Two Gardens: *The Prophet* by Kahlil Gibran (1923).

Fortnite Widow: References the video game Fortnite, created by Epic Games, a free-to-play cross-platform game played globally (created in 2016, as of 2022, approximately 24 million players log on to play daily).

Norwegian Air: Bronze sculpture Den lille Havfrau by Edvard Eriksen, bronze, (1913) inspired by HC Anderson's fairytale by same name, "The Little Mermaid."

Letter to the Eight-Year-Old Living There: *The Secret of the Old Clock* by Carolyn Keen (1930).

ACKNOWLEDGMENTS

Gratitude goes to the editors of the following journals and anthologies in which these poems or versions of them first appeared:

Aqueduct Press– "Couch Burning," *Climbing Lightly Through Forests: A Poetry Anthology Honoring Ursula K. Le Guin*

Bilingual / Borderless– "Snowflake Bentley" and "Full Moon Ghazal"

Blood Orange Review– "Bohemian Rhapsody"

Electric Rexroth– "Labor"

Ink Spot Press– "Stepfather" and "Dropping in the Eight," *A Year in Ink*

Journal of Applied Poetics– "Daughter by Candlelight"

Juked– "Berkeley Postcard"

Light-Journal– "Talking During the Eclipse"

Nimrod International Journal– "Free Box"

One– "Noctiluca"

Prime Number Magazine– "Hades"

Rockvale Review– "The Marriage Counselor Channels King Solomon" and "Two Gardens" (winner of Rockvale's time-themed poetry contest and residency)

San Diego Entertainment & Arts Guild, San Diego Poetry Annual & Garden Oak Press– "Moscow Road" (Honorable Mention, Kowit Prize) and "Bohemian Grove"

San Pedro River Review– "Silhouette"

Silver Birch Press– "Kolmer Gulch"

SWWIM– "My Daughter's Potato"

Tweetspeak Poetry— "Cooking Class," *Casual: a little book of jeans, poems, photos*

Whale Road Review— "Goat Milk Ice Cream"

Zoetic Press— "Rules for Consulting the Oracle" and "Duck"

ABOUT TANIA PRYPUTNIEWICZ

Tania Pryputniewicz is the author of the full-length poetry collection *November Butterfly* (Saddle Road Press, 2014), and *Heart's Compass Tarot: Discover Tarot Journaling and Create Your Own Cards* (Two Fine Crows Books, 2021).

Her poetry has appeared in numerous journals and anthologies including *America, We Call Your Name: Poems of Resistance and Resilience*; *Borderless / Bilingual*; *NILVX: A Book of Magic (Tarot Series)*; *Climbing Lightly Through Forests: A Poetry Anthology Honoring Ursula K. Le Guin*; *Nimrod*; *Poetry Flash*; *SWIMM*; *Whale Road Review*; and *Juked*; and is forthcoming in the anthology *Writing Through the Apocalypse: Pandemic Poetry and Prose* (Weeping Willow Press, 2023).

As teacher and tarot muse, Tania is a loving catalyst, helping others bring forth their stories through improvisation in poetry, memoir, art, and tarot. It is her joy to provide witness as other writers, artists, and seekers find confidence in their voices and arrive at a deeper sense of self-love and awareness.

A graduate of the Iowa Writers' Workshop, Tania teaches poetry and tarot-inspired writing classes for San Diego Writers, Ink and Antioch University's Continuing Education program as well as private courses through her website. She brings decades of experience reading tarot cards to her courses.

She is a reader for the International Memoir Writers Association's *Shaking the Tree* and *Memoir Showcase*, a reader for San Diego Writers, Ink's *A Year in Ink*, a poetry judge for the San Diego Writers Festival *KidsWrite!* Program, and a poetry peer reviewer for *Whale Road Review*.

She lives in Coronado, California with her husband, three children, one blue-eyed Siberian Husky named Sisu, and a formerly feral feline named Luna.

Connect with Tania through her website: taniapryputniewicz.com or on Instagram: @heartscompasstarot.

CPSIA information can be obtained
at www.ICGtesting.com
Printed in the USA
BVHW080156180123
656442BV00006B/843

9 781736 525876